Memories Of Johann Strauss: Twelve Most Famous Waltzes

Johann Strauss

Tales From The Vienna Woods

Geschichten Aus Dem Wiener Wald   *Légendes De La Forêt Viennoise*

Introduction
Tempo di Valse

JOHANN STRAUSS, Op. 325

Edward B. Marks Music Corporation

5

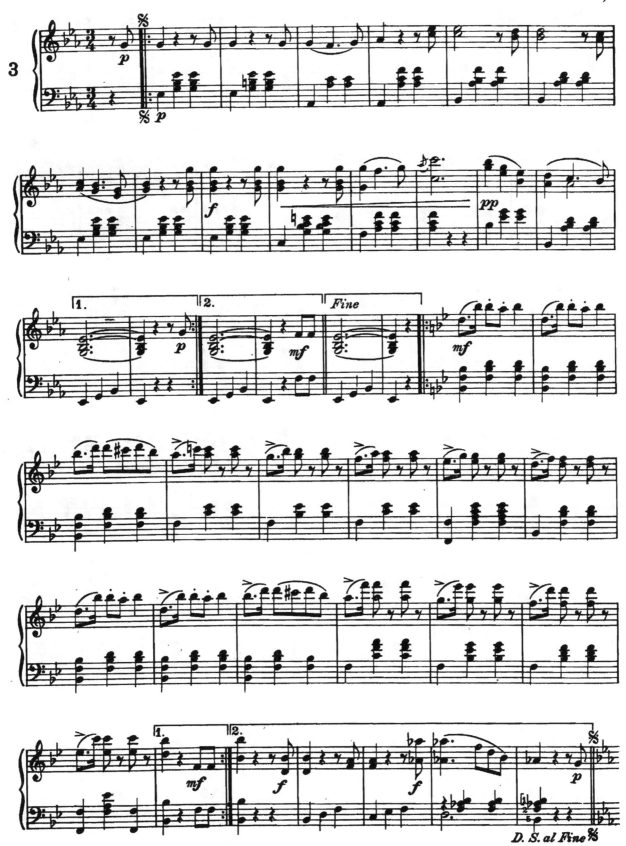

The Beautiful Blue Danube

An Der Schönen Blauen Donau   *Le Beau Danube Bleu*

INTRODUCTION.
Andantino

JOHANN STRAUSS, Op. **314**

Tempo di Valse.

7166-8

Dal Segno senza repetizione al Fine

7166-8

CODA

7166-8

Thousand And One Night

Tausend Und Eine Nacht *Les Mille Et Une Nuits*

JOHANN STRAUSS, Op. 346

Edward B. Marks Music Corporation

1

Trio

D.S. al Fine

3

Wine, Woman And Song

Wein, Weib Und Gesang   *Aimer, Boire, Chanter*

Johann Strauss, Op. 333

Edward B. Marks Music Corporation

WALTZ.

1.

2.

D. S. al Fine

32

Roses From The South

Rosen Aus Dem Süden   *Roses Du Midi*

Introduction
Andantino

JOHANN STRAUSS, Op. 388

Edward B. Marks Music Corporation

40

Sweetheart Waltz

From "The Gypsy Baron"

Schatz-Walzer　　　　　*Trésor Valse*

JOHANN STRAUSS, Op. 418

Introduction
Moderato

WALTZ.

Edward B. Marks Music Corporation

Voices Of Spring

Frühlingsstimmen　　　　　*Rêve De Printemps*

JOHANN STRAUSS, Op. 410

Edward B. Marks Music Corporation

54

Coda

58

Artist's Life

Künstlerleben   *La Vie D'Artiste*

Introduction
Andante moderato

JOHANN STRAUSS, Op. 316

Edward B. Marks Music Corporation

WALTZ.

1

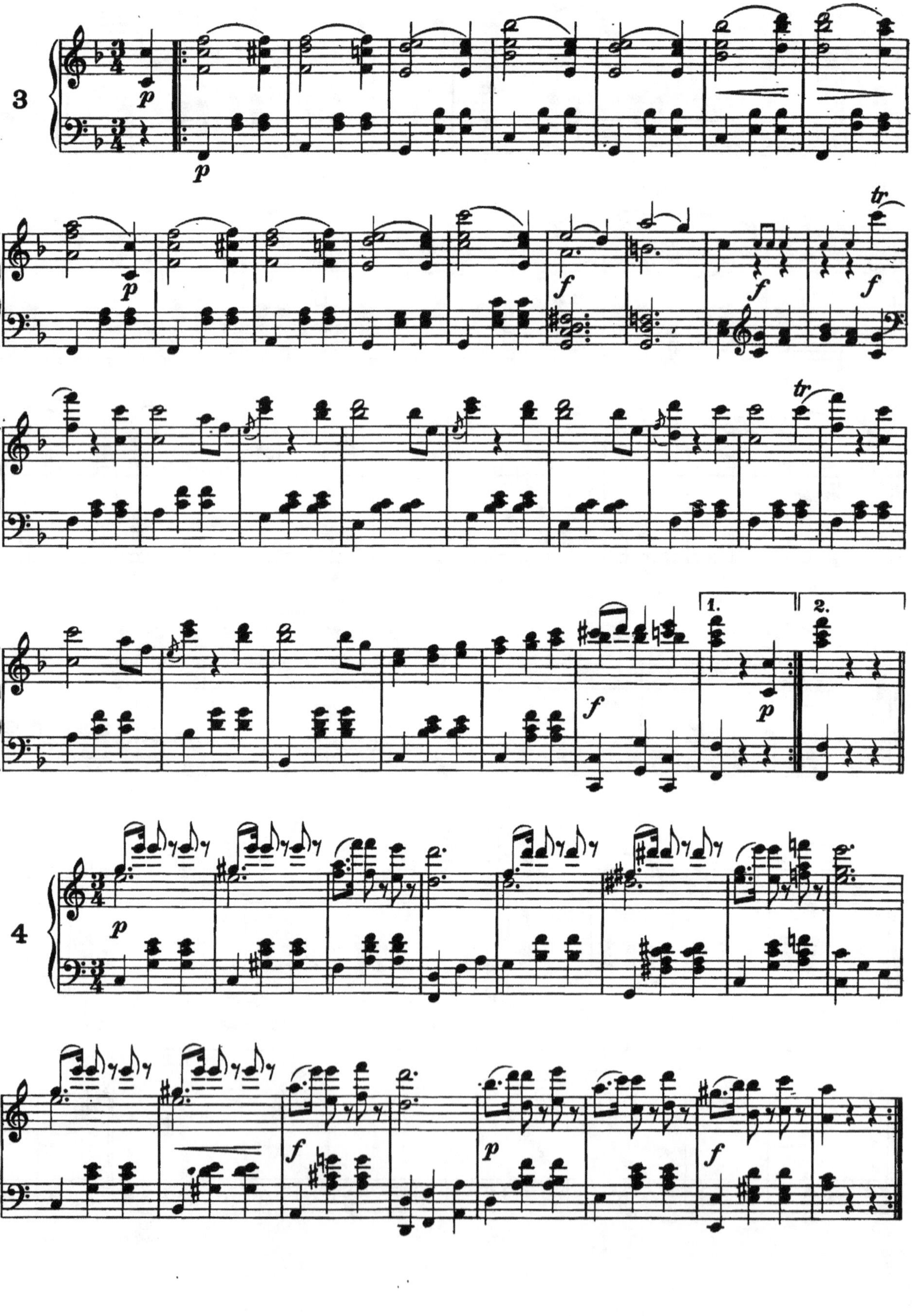
3
4

D. S.

You And You

From "The Bat"

Du Und Du　　　*Toi Et Toi*

Johann Strauss, Op. 367

Introduction
Moderato

Poco animato

Edward B. Marks Music Corporation

D.S. al fine

3

Coda

Vienna Life

Wiener Blut　　　　　　*Sang Viennois*

Introduction
Allegro moderato

JOHANN STRAUSS, Op. 354

Edward B. Marks Music Corporation

3

78

Kiss Waltz

Kuss-Walzer   *Les Baisers*

JOHANN STRAUSS, Op. 400

82

WALTZ

Emperor Waltz

Kaiser-Walzer   *Valse Imperiale*

Johann Strauss, Op. 437

Introduction
Slow March Tempo

Edward B. Marks Music Corporation

Tempo di Valse
ritard.

WALTZ
1.

mf ben legato ed espressivo

4.

Coda